Everybody *Wins!*

The Story of Special Olympics

by Cynthia Swain

PEARSON

Scott
Foresman

Editorial Offices: Glenview, Illinois • Parsippany, New Jersey • New York, New York
Sales Offices: Needham, Massachusetts • Duluth, Georgia • Glenview, Illinois
Coppell, Texas • Ontario, California • Mesa, Arizona

Joining In

Many people love playing sports. That includes people who are developmentally challenged. Such a disability is caused by the brain's inability to develop properly before birth or as a result of an injury after birth.

For a long time, people who were developmentally challenged weren't included in many activities that are part of daily life. Kids with intellectual disabilities often didn't go to school and were left out of sports. Many people didn't accept them.

Today, that's changed. People who are developmentally challenged can join in activities at school and in life. In sports, they can compete with other special athletes from around the world—in Special Olympics!

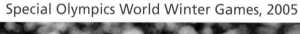

Special Olympics World Winter Games, 2005

Eunice Shriver:
Special Olympics Founder

Eunice Kennedy Shriver started Special Olympics. As a young woman, she saw up close how people with disabilities were treated. That's because her own sister, Rosemary Kennedy, had an intellectual disability. The Kennedy family was involved in politics. They were embarrassed by Rosemary's disability and kept it a secret.

Eunice wasn't embarrassed by her sister at all. When her brother, John F. Kennedy, was elected the 35th President of the United States in 1961, Eunice knew it was time to act.

Eunice convinced her family to admit to the public that their beloved sister and daughter had an intellectual disability. This was big news. It encouraged people all over the country to accept the intellectually **handicapped** in their own families and communities.

Eunice Kennedy Shriver (second from right) with her family

In the 1960s, Eunice and her husband started summer day camps across the country for children and adults with intellectual disabilities. When Eunice saw the campers playing outside, she realized that many of them were excellent athletes! She encouraged camp leaders to organize sports for the campers.

Then, the Chicago Park District came to Eunice with an idea. They asked if she would help them organize a citywide sports event for people with intellectual disabilities. They wanted to model the event on the Olympics.

Bicycling in a Special Olympics event

Chicago

Chicago was home to the first Special Olympics Summer Games.

Special Olympics Get Started

The First International Special Olympics Summer Games were held in Chicago in July 1968. One thousand people who are developmentally challenged came to compete. This was the start of something big.

Two years later, another Special Olympics in Chicago attracted more than twice as many athletes.

Then, in 1977, the First International Special Olympics Winter Games were held. Over 500 athletes competed in skiing and skating events.

In 1993, Special Olympics Winter Games went worldwide when the Games were held in Austria. More than 1,600 athletes from more than 50 countries participated.

Today, Special Olympics World Summer Games are held every four years. The Winter Games are held every four years as well.

Special Olympics give the developmentally challenged a chance to play their favorite sports and celebrate their victories.

Special Olympics Hit the Big Time

Today, Special Olympics is huge. In 2003, more than 6,000 athletes competed in Special Olympics World Summer Games in Ireland. It was the first time that the Summer Games were held outside the United States.

Iceland and USA teams play handball at the Special Olympics World Summer Games, Dublin, Ireland, 2003.

More than 150 countries participated in the 2003 Summer Games. The torch run started on June 4, in Athens, Greece. Dozens of law enforcement officers and 10 Special Olympics athletes joined in on the 9,000-mile, eight-day run. There were three routes across European cities that came together in Brussels. From there, the torch runners carried the flame to Dublin, Ireland.

The torch and runners got warm welcomes all across Europe. In Milan, Italy, over 15,000 people packed the streets to honor the athletes and the Games.

Special Olympics torch run, 2003

Loretta's Story

Some of the best athletes in Special Olympics come from the United States. Loretta Claiborne is one of them.

Loretta was born partially blind and developmentally challenged. She was not able to walk or talk until age four. She had surgery for her leg. She was teased at school for her awkward **gait,** suspended from high school, and fired from a job. Still, Loretta did not give up.

When Loretta learned to run, her life took a turn for the better. She started running marathons. So far, she's run in 25 of them! She finished in the top 100 women in the Boston Marathon—twice. But it was competing in Special Olympics that *really* changed her life.

President and Mrs. Clinton celebrate the 30th anniversary of Special Olympics with Loretta Claiborne.

Loretta became involved in Special Olympics as a kid. She won medals in many events, and she currently holds the women's record in her age group for the 5,000 meters at 17 minutes. She has competed in Special Olympics eight times, including the 2003 Games.

This amazing athlete also speaks out all across the world. She gives speeches to students about accepting differences in others. She has even had a movie made about her life, *The Loretta Claiborne Story.*

Newcomers to Special Olympics

Special Olympics athletes come from all over, even from countries that are very poor or at war. In 2003, five young athletes from Afghanistan competed for the first time in Ireland. They were all orphans.

Before 2001, Afghanistan was controlled by an oppressive government called the Taliban. People with disabilities were treated very poorly and sometimes even killed.

In 2001, the U.S. overthrew the Taliban. Now, the country is struggling to rebuild. Slowly, attitudes toward people with disabilities are changing.

The Afghani athletes were given their first pair of running shoes shortly before they came to the games. They had only one month to train, but their disadvantages didn't hold them back. One athlete, 11-year-old Amin Amin, won gold medals in the 50-meter and 25-meter relays.

"It's a great opportunity for them to experience this feeling," said their coach, Nasrullah Ibrahimzay.

Ireland

Ireland was the site of the 2003 Special Olympics Summer Games.

In 1995, the Special Olympics were held in Connecticut.

Afghanistan

Brave Competitors

Today all athletes take the Special Olympics Athlete Oath: "Let me win, but if I cannot win—let me be brave in the attempt."

Luis Canel is an athlete from Guatemala. He competed in the Summer Games in Ireland in 2003. He is brave—and he is a winner.

Getting to the Olympics was tough for Luis. His mother died in 1995. His father abandoned the family. Luis loved his sport and knew he could do well at the Summer Games, but he couldn't afford a bike.

Luis's friends raised money to buy him a bike. When he got to Ireland, he made them all proud. He won a gold medal for bike racing in the 5 kilometer time trial, and he won two bronze medals in the 1 kilometer and 10 kilometer time trials.

Liinah Bukenya, a 12-year-old swimmer from Uganda, overcame an impressive obstacle as well. Eleven months before the Summer Games, she didn't even know how to swim!

"I thought maybe I might get a silver," Liinah said during the Games, "but this morning I said to myself that even if I didn't get anything I would be brave."

Liinah beat her own expectations. She won the gold medal in the 50-meter backstroke!

The Biggest Challenge

People who have intellectual disabilities sometimes have physical disabilities as well. They might need a **wheelchair** to get around. Some might need **artificial** limbs. Because of this, physical educators, physical **therapists,** and recreational therapists developed the Special Olympics Motor Activities Training Program (MATP). MATP gives *all* athletes a chance to shine.

All Special Olympics athletes train hard. This is especially true for MATP athletes. They work to strengthen their arms and shoulders, back and **abdomen,** and feet and legs.

MATP events may seem easy to you, but for the athletes who participate in them, they require as much practice and determination as any Olympic event. At the 2003 Special Olympics World Summer Games in Ireland, the MATP events were the bean bag lift, ball kick, wide beam and bench, ball lift (small), ball lift (large), ball push, and log roll.

One of the participants in the bean bag lift at the 2003 Games was Gary Durcan, age 14. Cheering from the audience encouraged a hesitant Gary to pick up a yellow bean bag and toss it into the basket. "Gary can't communicate, but we can see the excitement in his eyes," said his father.

One of the events at the Summer Games is the softball throw.

Everybody Wins

For Special Olympics athletes, it is the spirit—
not the score—that is important. Runner Loretta
Claiborne says, "What's important is that you throw
a softball when before you couldn't throw a softball.
You do better than the last time. That's what
counts." Gold, silver, and bronze medals are awarded
at Special Olympics events, but all athletes receive a
ribbon or medal for participating.

Fair play also counts. That's why athletes are placed in divisions based on their ability. All are given a fair chance to compete and win.

Athletes also get a chance to meet famous and respected people. Former South African president Nelson Mandela spoke at the Special Olympics World Games in Dublin. The President of Poland helped award medals.

Join in the Fun!

Do Special Olympics sound like fun? They aren't *just* for people who are developmentally challenged. In fact, there are many ways for athletes without intellectual disabilities and others to join in.

Unified Sports are sports that team up athletes with and without disabilities. These teams also compete in Special Olympics.

Michael Kennet is the Unified Sports partner of Nic Jones. They are both from Great Britain and compete in sailing. Michael has an intellectual disability, and having a friend like Nic helps him compete at his best. Michael and Nic have known each other for four years. It's been a rewarding friendship for both of them.

Many people volunteer during the World Games. There are over 500,000 Special Olympics volunteers from all over. They include adults and kids, amateur and professional athletes, teachers, coaches, and retirees. Even companies get involved.

There's also a program just for students, called The Global Youth Summit, which includes people with and without disabilities. At the 2003 Games, they met to discuss discrimination against people who are developmentally challenged. The group was highlighted on TV shows and in newspapers all around the world. One Summit member, 13-year old Kamna Prem from New Dehli, India, voiced the group's goal: "At the end, attitudes will change toward people with mental challenges."

What's Next?

Today, over 1.4 million people who are developmentally challenged compete in Special Olympics training programs, clubs, or events. Special Olympics have come a long way since they started in 1963!

In 2007, Special Olympics World Summer Games will be held in Shanghai, China. Fans will be wowed by amazing athletic feats. Athletes will walk to the medals podium proudly to honor their home countries. Best of all, people who who are developmentally challenged will have the opportunity to play fair, compete, and win.

Opening ceremony, Special Olympics World Summer Games,
Dublin, Ireland, 2003

Glossary

abdomen *n.* the part of the body between the thorax and the pelvis, roughly corresponding to the stomach area

artificial *adj.* man-made

gait *n.* manner of walking

handicapped *n.* person or persons having a physical or intellectual disability that substantially limits activity

therapist *n.* a person trained in methods of treatment and rehabilitation that do not use drugs or surgery

wheelchair *n.* a chair mounted on wheels for the use of disabled people